The Entrepreneur's Playbook

Insider Tips and Tactics for Launching and Scaling Your Business

GALE DAY

Copyright 2024 by GALE DAY
All Rights Reserved

Table of Contents

Chapter 1

Introduction

Welcome to The Entrepreneur's Playbook
Embarking on the entrepreneurial journey is a thrilling and challenging adventure, filled with both opportunities and obstacles. As you open this book, you're taking the first step towards transforming your ideas into reality, navigating through the complexities of building and scaling a business. This playbook is designed to be your companion and guide, offering insights, strategies, and practical advice to help you succeed.

Starting a business is much like preparing for a marathon. It requires preparation, endurance, and a clear strategy. You wouldn't start running 26.2 miles without training and a plan; similarly, diving into entrepreneurship without understanding the landscape can lead to unnecessary setbacks. This chapter aims to set the stage for your entrepreneurial journey, providing the foundation upon which you can build and grow your business.

One of the initial steps in your journey is understanding the importance of mindset. The entrepreneurial mindset is characterized by resilience, adaptability, and a willingness to learn. Challenges and failures are inevitable, but how you respond to them will determine your success. Embrace a growth mindset, where you view setbacks as learning opportunities rather than insurmountable obstacles.

This perspective will keep you motivated and persistent, even when the going gets tough.

Having a clear vision and purpose is crucial. Your vision is your North Star, guiding every decision and action you take. It's not just about what you want to achieve, but why you want to achieve it. A strong, compelling vision will inspire you and your team, and it will help attract investors, customers, and partners who share your passion and belief in your mission.

Equally important is setting realistic and achievable goals. Break down your vision into smaller, actionable steps. These goals will serve as milestones, helping you measure progress and stay on track. When setting goals, use the SMART criteria – Specific, Measurable, Achievable, Relevant, and Time-bound. This approach ensures that your goals are clear and attainable, providing a roadmap for your journey.

Understanding your market is another critical aspect of entrepreneurship. Before investing time and resources into developing a product or service, you need to validate your business idea. This involves researching your target market, understanding their needs and pain points, and analyzing the competitive landscape. Market research will help you identify opportunities and gaps, allowing you to tailor your offering to meet the demands of your potential customers.

Conducting thorough market research involves several steps. Start by identifying your target audience – who are they, where do they live, what are their demographics and psychographics? Use surveys, interviews, and focus groups to gather qualitative data about their preferences, behaviors, and challenges. Additionally, analyze industry reports, market trends, and competitor data to gain a comprehensive understanding of the market dynamics.

Once you have validated your idea, the next step is to develop a minimum viable product (MVP). An MVP is a simplified version of your product or service that allows you to test your concept with real users. The goal is to gather feedback, validate assumptions, and iterate based on user input. This lean approach helps you avoid the pitfalls of over-investing in a product that may not resonate with your market.

Creating a business plan is essential for laying the groundwork for your venture. A well-crafted business plan outlines your business model, target market, competitive analysis, marketing strategy, operational plan, and financial projections. It serves as a blueprint, guiding your actions and decisions. Moreover, a solid business plan is crucial when seeking funding from investors or financial institutions, as it demonstrates the viability and potential of your business.

Securing funding is often one of the biggest challenges for entrepreneurs. There are several avenues you can explore, including bootstrapping, angel investors, venture capitalists, small business loans, and crowdfunding. Each option has its pros and cons, and the right choice depends on your business model, stage of development, and funding needs. Bootstrapping, for example, allows you to retain full control of your business, but it may limit your growth potential. On the other hand, venture capital can provide significant resources, but it often comes with the expectation of rapid growth and a loss of some control.

Managing cash flow is critical for the survival and growth of your business. Cash flow problems are one of the leading causes of business failure. Ensure you have a clear understanding of your financials, including revenue streams, expenses, and profit margins. Implementing sound financial management practices, such as budgeting, forecasting, and regular financial reviews, will help you maintain a healthy cash flow and make informed decisions.

Building a brand is more than just creating a logo or a tagline. Your brand is the identity of your business, reflecting your values, mission, and the promise you make to your customers. A strong brand differentiates you from competitors and creates a lasting impression in the minds of your customers. Start by defining your brand identity – what do you stand for, what are your core values, and how do you want to be perceived? Craft a compelling brand story that resonates with your audience and communicates your unique value proposition.

Establishing an online presence is vital in today's digital age. Your website is often the first point of contact for potential customers, so it's crucial that it reflects your brand effectively. Invest in a professionally designed website that is user-friendly, mobile-responsive, and optimized for search engines. Your website should clearly communicate who you are, what you offer, and how customers can benefit from your products or services.

What You Will Learn

Embarking on the entrepreneurial journey can feel like navigating an uncharted territory. It's a path marked by both exhilarating victories and daunting challenges. This book serves as your compass, offering the insights and strategies essential to transforming your business ideas into a thriving enterprise. As you delve into these pages, you'll gain a comprehensive understanding of the critical aspects of entrepreneurship, from ideation to execution, and everything in between.

First and foremost, you'll learn how to validate your business idea. Many entrepreneurs fall into the trap of assuming their idea is brilliant without thoroughly testing it in the real world. This book will guide you through understanding market needs and conducting effective market research. You'll discover how to analyze your competition and create a compelling value proposition that sets your offering apart. Testing your idea with minimum viable products (MVP) is a crucial step, and you'll learn actionable techniques to gather feedback and refine your concept before fully committing resources.

Developing a solid business plan is another fundamental skill you'll acquire. A well-crafted business plan is more than a document; it's a strategic tool that outlines your vision, goals, and the roadmap to achieve them. You'll explore why a business plan is essential and what elements it should include. From setting realistic goals and milestones to developing financial projections, you'll understand how to create a comprehensive plan that not only guides your actions but also attracts potential investors and stakeholders.

Securing funding is often one of the most challenging aspects of starting a business. This book will equip you with knowledge about various funding options, including bootstrapping, approaching angel investors and venture capitalists, applying for small business loans, and leveraging crowdfunding strategies. You'll learn how to craft compelling pitches and proposals that resonate with investors. Additionally, managing cash flow and budgets effectively will be covered, ensuring you have the financial acumen to sustain and grow your business.

Building a strong brand is pivotal in today's competitive marketplace. You'll delve into the intricacies of defining your brand identity and creating a brand story that resonates with your target audience. From designing a memorable logo and visuals to establishing an online presence, you'll gain insights into how to make your brand stand out. Leveraging social media for brand growth is another critical area you'll explore, learning how to engage with your audience and build a loyal customer base.

Product or service development is at the heart of your business operations. Understanding product development cycles, from ideation to launch, is crucial. You'll learn how to prototype and test your product, source materials and suppliers effectively, and implement quality assurance measures. Gathering user feedback and iterating based on real-world usage will help you refine your offering and ensure it meets customer expectations.

Effective marketing and sales strategies are essential for driving revenue and growth. You'll discover how to create a comprehensive marketing plan that aligns with your business goals. Understanding your target audience is key, and you'll learn techniques to segment and reach your ideal customers. Digital marketing tactics, such as SEO, content marketing, and social media advertising, will be covered in detail. Building a sales funnel and measuring marketing ROI will help you optimize your efforts and maximize returns.

Building a winning team is another critical component of business success. You'll explore how to identify key roles and responsibilities within your organization and recruit top talent. Fostering a positive company culture is essential for employee satisfaction and retention. You'll learn leadership and team management skills that inspire and motivate your team. Employee retention strategies, including professional development and competitive compensation, will also be discussed, ensuring you can build and maintain a high-performing team.

Throughout your journey, you'll encounter various challenges and obstacles. This book will equip you with problem-solving skills and resilience strategies to overcome these hurdles. You'll learn how to stay adaptable in a constantly changing business landscape and how to pivot when necessary. Building a support network of mentors, advisors, and peers will provide you with valuable guidance and encouragement.

Understanding the legal and regulatory aspects of running a business is crucial. You'll gain insights into choosing the right business structure, registering your business, and complying with local, state, and federal regulations. Protecting your intellectual property and understanding contracts and agreements will also be covered, ensuring you can safeguard your business interests.

Customer satisfaction and retention are vital for long-term success. You'll learn how to create exceptional customer experiences and build strong relationships with your clients. Implementing feedback loops and continuously improving your product or service based on customer input will help you maintain a competitive edge.

As you scale your business, you'll encounter new challenges and opportunities. This book will guide you through growth strategies, including expanding your product line, entering new markets, and scaling operations. You'll learn how to manage growing pains and maintain the quality and consistency of your offerings. Strategic partnerships and alliances can also play a significant role in scaling, and you'll explore how to identify and leverage these opportunities.

Financial management remains a critical aspect as your business grows. You'll delve deeper into advanced financial planning, including managing investments, optimizing tax strategies, and planning for long-term sustainability. Understanding financial statements and key performance indicators (KPIs) will help you make informed decisions and drive business growth.

Innovation and continuous improvement are essential for staying relevant in a dynamic market. You'll learn how to foster a culture of innovation within your organization. Encouraging creativity and experimentation can lead to breakthrough ideas and improvements. You'll explore techniques for brainstorming, ideation, and implementing new technologies or processes that can give your business a competitive edge. Embracing change and staying ahead of industry trends will be vital in maintaining your position in the market.

Who This Book Is For
Navigating the intricate maze of entrepreneurship can be a daunting task. This book is designed to serve as a beacon for a diverse audience, each with unique aspirations and challenges. Whether you're an aspiring entrepreneur with a nascent idea, an established business owner seeking to scale, or someone contemplating a career shift, this guide is tailored to meet your needs and propel you towards success.

For the aspiring entrepreneur, this book offers a treasure trove of insights and practical advice. You may have a spark of an idea but are unsure how to transform it into a viable business. This book demystifies the process, breaking down each step from ideation to execution. You'll learn how to validate your concept, conduct market research, and develop a solid business plan. It's a roadmap that turns uncertainty into actionable steps, providing the confidence and clarity needed to take that first leap.

Established business owners will find this book invaluable for scaling their ventures. Running a business can often feel like being on a treadmill, with constant demands and little time to strategize for growth. This book delves into advanced strategies for expanding your market reach, optimizing operations, and enhancing customer engagement. You'll discover new ways to innovate, streamline processes, and maintain a competitive edge. It's about moving beyond survival mode and positioning your business for long-term success.

Career changers contemplating entrepreneurship will also find this book a guiding light. Transitioning from a stable job to starting your own business is a significant decision, fraught with risks and uncertainties. This book addresses those concerns head-on, offering insights into financial planning, risk management, and the psychological aspects of such a shift. You'll learn how to leverage your existing skills and experiences in the entrepreneurial world, making the transition smoother and more manageable.

Students and recent graduates are another key audience for this book. In today's dynamic job market, entrepreneurship is increasingly seen as a viable path straight out of academia. This book provides the foundational knowledge necessary to start a business right after graduation. From understanding the basics of business operations to leveraging modern digital tools, students will gain a comprehensive overview of what it takes to launch and sustain a business in today's competitive environment.

Freelancers and gig economy workers will also benefit from the strategies outlined in this book. If you're working independently but looking to formalize your business and create a more stable income stream, this guide can help. You'll learn how to build a brand, market your services effectively, and manage your finances. The goal is to transition from being a solo operator to running a structured and profitable business.

Non-profit founders and social entrepreneurs will find tailored advice that addresses the unique challenges of mission-driven ventures. Balancing social impact with financial sustainability requires a nuanced approach. This book delves into strategies for fundraising, building a volunteer base, and measuring impact. It's about creating a business model that not only achieves your social goals but also ensures long-term viability.

Even those who are simply curious about entrepreneurship will find value in this book. Understanding the entrepreneurial mindset and the mechanics of starting and running a business can be incredibly enriching, even if you never start your own venture. It cultivates a spirit of innovation and problem-solving that can be applied in various aspects of life and career.

This book also speaks to those who have faced setbacks or failures in their entrepreneurial journey. Failure is often an integral part of the entrepreneurial process, and it's crucial to learn from it rather than be deterred. This guide provides strategies for analyzing what went wrong, how to pivot effectively, and how to build resilience. It's about turning setbacks into stepping stones and using those experiences to forge a stronger path forward.

Seasoned professionals who are mentoring or advising startups will find this book a useful resource. The comprehensive coverage of topics provides mentors with a structured approach to guide their mentees. It ensures that they're providing well-rounded advice that covers all critical aspects of starting and scaling a business.

Investors and venture capitalists can also gain insights from this book. Understanding the entrepreneur's journey, the challenges they face, and the strategies that drive success can inform better investment decisions. It provides a lens through which to evaluate potential investments and support portfolio companies more effectively.

Lastly, this book is for anyone passionate about innovation and creating value. Entrepreneurship is not just about starting a business; it's about identifying opportunities, creating solutions, and making a difference. This book celebrates that spirit and provides the tools and knowledge to turn passion into action.

In essence, this book is a comprehensive guide designed to meet the needs of a diverse audience. It recognizes that the path to entrepreneurship is not one-size-fits-all and tailors its advice to various stages and scenarios. Whether you're just starting out, looking to scale, transitioning from another career, or seeking to make a social impact, this book provides the insights and strategies necessary to navigate the entrepreneurial landscape successfully. It's about empowering you with the knowledge and confidence to take control of your entrepreneurial journey and achieve your goals.

Entrepreneurship is often synonymous with risk, resilience, and relentless pursuit of innovation. For those who have experienced setbacks or failures, this book serves as a crucial guide to bouncing back stronger. Failure in business can be disheartening, but it is also a powerful teacher. This book delves into how to conduct a post-mortem analysis of your failed ventures, identifying what went wrong and what could have been done differently. By understanding these nuances, you can pivot your strategy, avoid past mistakes, and rebuild your enterprise on a more solid foundation.

How to Use This Book

Embarking on the journey of entrepreneurship is akin to setting sail in uncharted waters. This book is your compass, designed to guide you through the complexities and challenges of building and growing a business. Understanding how to navigate this book effectively will maximize its value and ensure you leverage its insights to their fullest potential.

First and foremost, approach this book with an open mind. The entrepreneurial landscape is ever-evolving, and flexibility is key. As you read, be prepared to adapt the strategies and advice to your unique context. While the principles outlined here are universally applicable, the specific application will depend on your individual circumstances, industry, and goals. This book is not a rigid blueprint but rather a flexible framework to guide your decision-making and problem-solving processes.

Start by familiarizing yourself with the table of contents. This will give you a comprehensive overview of the topics covered and help you identify the sections most relevant to your current stage. Whether you're in the ideation phase, ready to launch, or looking to scale, knowing where to find the information you need will save time and enhance your learning experience.

As you delve into the chapters, take notes and highlight key points. Entrepreneurship is an active process, and engaging with the material will deepen your understanding. Use a notebook or digital tool to jot down ideas, questions, and reflections. This practice not only reinforces learning but also creates a personalized resource you can refer back to as you progress.

One of the most valuable aspects of this book is its emphasis on practical, actionable advice. As you read, identify specific actions you can take and create a to-do list. Break down larger goals into manageable tasks and set deadlines for completion. This approach will help you maintain momentum and ensure that you're consistently moving forward.

Throughout the book, you'll encounter real-world examples and case studies. These stories illustrate the principles in action and provide valuable lessons. Pay close attention to these examples, as they offer insights into how successful entrepreneurs navigate challenges and seize opportunities. Reflect on how these lessons apply to your own venture and consider how you can adopt similar strategies.

Networking and building relationships are crucial components of entrepreneurial success. This book emphasizes the importance of connecting with others in the entrepreneurial ecosystem. As you read, note any suggestions or strategies related to networking and make a plan to implement them. Attend industry events, join online forums, and reach out to potential mentors or collaborators. Building a strong network will provide support, open doors, and offer fresh perspectives.

Financial literacy is another critical area covered in this book. Understanding the financial aspects of running a business is essential for making informed decisions and ensuring long-term viability. Pay close attention to chapters on budgeting, funding, and financial management. Use the tools and templates provided to create detailed financial plans and projections. Regularly review and update these documents to stay on top of your financial health.

Marketing and branding are integral to business success, and this book offers a wealth of strategies in these areas. As you read, think about your target audience and how you can effectively reach and engage them. Develop a marketing plan that outlines your key messages, channels, and tactics. Experiment with different approaches and measure their effectiveness. Be prepared to iterate and refine your strategy based on feedback and results.

The entrepreneurial journey is often fraught with challenges and setbacks. This book provides guidance on building resilience and maintaining a positive mindset. Take to heart the advice on coping with failure, managing stress, and staying motivated. Entrepreneurship requires perseverance and the ability to bounce back from adversity. Cultivate a growth mindset and view challenges as opportunities to learn and grow.

Innovation and creativity are at the heart of entrepreneurship. This book encourages you to think outside the box and continuously seek new ways to create value. Embrace a culture of experimentation and be willing to take calculated risks. Use the frameworks and techniques provided to brainstorm ideas, evaluate opportunities, and develop innovative solutions. Remember that innovation is not a one-time event but an ongoing process.

While this book is a comprehensive guide, it's important to supplement your learning with additional resources. Stay informed about industry trends, read widely, and seek out other experts in the field. Join professional organizations, attend workshops, and participate in online courses. The more knowledge and skills you acquire, the better equipped you'll be to navigate the entrepreneurial landscape.

Reflection and self-assessment are key components of effective learning. Periodically review your progress and evaluate the impact of the strategies you've implemented. Identify what's working well and where there are opportunities for improvement. Use the self-assessment tools provided in this book to gauge your strengths and weaknesses. Set aside time for regular reflection and goal setting to ensure you're on track and making meaningful progress.

Collaboration is another powerful tool in the entrepreneurial toolkit. Throughout this book, you'll find references to the importance of building a strong team and leveraging the skills and expertise of others. Whether you're working with co-founders, employees, or external partners, effective collaboration can drive innovation and accelerate growth. Focus on building a team that shares your vision and complements your strengths. Foster a culture of open communication, mutual respect, and continuous learning.

Adaptability is a recurring theme in this book. The ability to pivot and adjust your strategies in response to changing circumstances is crucial for long-term success. Stay attuned to market trends, customer feedback, and technological advancements. Be ready to shift your approach when necessary, and view change as an opportunity rather than a setback. This book provides guidelines on how to stay agile and responsive, ensuring your business remains relevant and competitive.

The Journey Ahead
Embarking on the path of entrepreneurship is akin to setting out on a vast, unpredictable adventure. The journey ahead is filled with highs and lows, unexpected challenges, and rewarding triumphs. Understanding what to expect and how to navigate

this landscape is crucial for any aspiring entrepreneur.

Imagine standing at the edge of a dense forest, knowing that on the other side lies the realization of your dreams. The path through the forest is not clearly marked, and each step requires careful consideration. The journey of building a business is much the same. It starts with a vision, a spark of an idea that ignites your passion. But turning that idea into a successful venture requires planning, resilience, and a willingness to learn and adapt.

The first step on this journey is to clearly define your vision. What do you hope to achieve with your business? What problems are you solving, and for whom? A well-defined vision serves as your North Star, guiding your decisions and keeping you focused on your long-term goals. Take the time to articulate this vision in a mission statement that succinctly captures the essence of your business.

With your vision in place, the next step is to conduct thorough research. Understanding your market, competitors, and potential customers is essential. This research will inform every aspect of your business plan, from product development to marketing strategies. Dive deep into industry reports, customer surveys, and competitive analysis. Gather as much information as possible to make informed decisions and identify your unique value proposition.

As you gather data, begin crafting a comprehensive business plan. This document will serve as your roadmap, outlining your business model, target market, competitive landscape, marketing and sales

strategies, operational plan, and financial projections.
A well-thought-out business plan not only helps you
clarify your ideas but also becomes a vital tool when
seeking funding from investors or financial
institutions.

Funding is often one of the biggest hurdles for new
entrepreneurs. There are various options to consider,
from bootstrapping and personal savings to loans,
grants, and venture capital. Each option has its pros
and cons, and the best choice depends on your specific
circumstances and business model. Carefully evaluate
each funding source, considering factors like the
amount of capital needed, repayment terms, and the
potential impact on your business equity.

Once you secure funding, the real work begins.
Building a team is one of the most critical aspects of
your journey. Surround yourself with individuals who
complement your skills and share your vision. Look
for people who are not only talented but also
passionate about your mission. A strong, cohesive
team can overcome challenges and drive the business
forward.

With your team in place, focus on developing your
product or service. This phase requires a balance of
creativity and practicality. Strive for excellence, but
also be mindful of time and resources. Utilize
feedback from potential customers to refine your
offering and ensure it meets their needs. Remember,
the goal is to create something that provides real value
and stands out in the market.

Marketing and sales strategies are essential for
reaching your target audience and driving revenue.

Develop a marketing plan that encompasses various channels such as social media, email marketing, content marketing, and paid advertising. Each channel has its strengths, and a diversified approach ensures you reach a broader audience. For sales, build a process that is customer-centric, focusing on understanding and addressing their needs.

As your business grows, operational efficiency becomes increasingly important. Implement systems and processes that streamline operations, improve productivity, and reduce costs. Technology can be a powerful ally in this regard, offering tools for project management, customer relationship management, and financial tracking. Regularly review and optimize these processes to ensure they continue to support your growth.

Financial management is another critical aspect of your journey. Keep a close eye on your cash flow, expenses, and profitability. Accurate financial records and reports provide insights into your business's health and help you make informed decisions. Consider working with a financial advisor or accountant to ensure your financial practices are sound and compliant with regulations.

The journey of entrepreneurship is not without its challenges. Setbacks and failures are inevitable, but they also present opportunities for learning and growth. Build resilience by maintaining a positive mindset and viewing each challenge as a stepping stone toward success. Seek advice from mentors, peers, and professionals who can offer guidance and support during difficult times.

Networking is a powerful tool for entrepreneurs. Building relationships with other business owners, industry experts, and potential customers can open doors to new opportunities, partnerships, and insights. Attend industry events, join professional organizations, and participate in online forums. Networking not only expands your knowledge but also creates a support system that can be invaluable on your journey.

As you navigate the ups and downs of entrepreneurship, don't forget to take care of yourself. Balancing work and personal life is essential for long-term sustainability. Prioritize self-care, set boundaries, and make time for activities that recharge you. A healthy, well-balanced lifestyle enhances your creativity, decision-making, and overall well-being.

Innovation and adaptability are key to staying relevant in a constantly changing market. Continuously seek ways to improve your products, services, and business processes. Stay informed about industry trends and technological advancements, and be willing to pivot when necessary. Embrace a culture of experimentation within your team, encouraging them to explore new ideas and approaches. This mindset not only drives innovation but also keeps your business agile and competitive.

Chapter 2: Validating Your Business Idea

You've got an exciting business idea, and the vision is clear in your mind. The next crucial step is validating that idea to ensure it has the potential to succeed in the real world. Many entrepreneurs skip this phase, eager to jump straight into building their product or service, but validation is what separates a great idea from a viable business. It's about gathering evidence that there is a demand for your product, that your solution resonates with potential customers, and that you're on the right path before investing significant time and resources.

Start by clearly defining your target market. Who are the people or businesses that will benefit the most from your product or service? Understanding your audience is key to validation. Create detailed customer personas that include demographics, behaviors, needs, and pain points. The more specific you are, the easier it will be to tailor your validation efforts.

Next, engage in market research. This involves both qualitative and quantitative methods. Begin with qualitative research to gather in-depth insights. Conduct interviews with potential customers to understand their needs and challenges. Use open-ended questions to encourage detailed responses. Attend industry events, join relevant online forums, and participate in discussions to gauge interest and gather feedback. These conversations will provide valuable insight into whether your idea addresses a real problem and how it can be refined to better meet customer needs.

Quantitative research is equally important. This involves collecting numerical data to validate the scale of demand for your product. Surveys can be an effective tool here. Design a survey with a mix of multiple-choice and open-ended questions that target your customer personas. Distribute the survey through various channels such as social media, email lists, and industry groups. Analyze the responses to identify patterns and quantify interest.

Competitor analysis is another critical aspect of validation. Identify existing businesses offering similar products or services. Study their offerings, pricing, marketing strategies, and customer reviews. This analysis will help you understand the competitive landscape and identify gaps that your business can fill. It can also provide insights into what customers like and dislike about existing solutions, guiding you in refining your own offering.

Once you have a solid understanding of your market and competition, it's time to test your idea with a minimum viable product (MVP). An MVP is a simplified version of your product that includes only the core features necessary to solve the main problem for your target audience. The goal is to get your MVP into the hands of users as quickly as possible to gather feedback and learn from their experiences.

Developing an MVP doesn't mean cutting corners; it means focusing on what's essential. For example, if you're creating a software application, build the basic functionalities that address the primary pain points. If it's a physical product, create a prototype that demonstrates how it works. The key is to deliver something functional that allows you to test your assumptions.

Launch your MVP to a small, targeted audience. This could be through a soft launch, beta testing, or a limited release. Monitor how users interact with your product and collect feedback through surveys, interviews, and analytics. Pay close attention to their behavior: Are they using the product as you intended? What features do they find most valuable? What issues or frustrations do they encounter?

Analyzing this feedback is crucial for iterating on your product. Use the insights gained to make informed decisions about what features to add, remove, or improve. This iterative process helps you refine your product based on real user experiences, increasing the likelihood of success when you launch to a broader audience.

In addition to user feedback, measure key performance indicators (KPIs) to assess your MVP's success. These might include metrics like user engagement, conversion rates, customer acquisition costs, and retention rates. Tracking these metrics provides quantitative evidence of your product's viability and helps you identify areas for improvement.

Customer validation doesn't stop with the MVP. As you continue to develop and grow your business, ongoing validation is essential. Regularly engage with your customers to understand their evolving needs and gather feedback on new features or changes. This continuous loop of feedback and iteration ensures that your product remains relevant and valuable.

Another powerful validation tool is the pre-order or crowdfunding campaign. Platforms like Kickstarter and Indiegogo allow you to present your idea to a large audience and gauge interest through pre-orders. A successful campaign not only provides funding but also validates that there is a market willing to pay for your product. It demonstrates demand and can attract additional investors or partners.

Building a community around your product can also enhance validation efforts. Engage with potential customers through social media, blogs, and forums. Create valuable content that addresses their needs and showcases your expertise. Building a loyal following helps you gather feedback, generate buzz, and establish a customer base before your official launch.

Validation is not a one-time task but an ongoing process. Markets evolve, customer preferences change, and new competitors emerge. Staying attuned to these shifts and continuously validating your business idea ensures that you adapt and remain competitive. It requires a mindset of curiosity, openness to feedback, and a willingness to pivot when necessary.

Throughout this journey, maintain a balance between optimism and realism. Believe in your vision, but be prepared to face hard truths when the data suggests that changes are necessary. Validation is about finding that sweet spot where your passion meets market demand. It's about being flexible and resilient, ready to tweak, adjust, or even overhaul your initial idea based on what you learn.

Understanding Market Needs

Understanding market needs is a crucial step in the journey of any entrepreneur. It lays the foundation for a successful business by ensuring that your product or service addresses a genuine demand. This process begins with a deep dive into your potential customers' lives, problems, and preferences. The more you understand about your market, the better you can tailor your offerings to meet their needs effectively.

One of the first steps in understanding market needs is identifying your target audience. This involves segmenting the market based on various factors such as demographics, psychographics, behavior, and geography. Demographic factors include age, gender, income level, education, and occupation, while psychographics delve into interests, values, lifestyles, and personality traits. Behavioral segmentation looks at purchasing habits, brand loyalty, and product usage, whereas geographic segmentation considers location, climate, and cultural preferences.

Creating detailed customer personas helps bring your target audience to life. These personas are fictional representations of your ideal customers. For instance, if you're launching a fitness app, you might create personas like "Busy Brenda," a working mother looking for quick, effective workouts, or "Fitness Fanatic Frank," a young professional seeking advanced training programs. These personas help you visualize and empathize with your customers, guiding your marketing and product development decisions.

To gather insights into your market, start with primary research. This involves collecting data directly from potential customers through surveys, interviews, focus groups, and observations. Surveys are a cost-effective way to reach a large audience and gather quantitative data. Design your surveys to include a mix of closed-ended questions for statistical analysis and open-ended questions for qualitative insights. Platforms like SurveyMonkey or Google Forms can facilitate this process.

Interviews and focus groups provide deeper, qualitative understanding. Conduct one-on-one interviews to explore individual customer experiences, preferences, and pain points. Focus groups, on the other hand, allow you to observe group dynamics and gather diverse perspectives in a moderated setting. When conducting interviews or focus groups, ask open-ended questions that encourage detailed responses, and listen actively to uncover underlying needs and motivations.

Secondary research complements your primary research by providing existing data from reliable sources. This includes industry reports, market studies, academic journals, government publications, and news articles. Organizations like Nielsen, Gartner, and McKinsey regularly publish valuable market insights. Analyze this data to identify trends, market size, growth potential, and competitive landscape.

Competitor analysis is another essential aspect of understanding market needs. Identify your direct and indirect competitors and study their offerings, pricing, marketing strategies, and customer reviews. Tools like

SWOT analysis (Strengths, Weaknesses, Opportunities, Threats) can help you systematically evaluate your competitors. Understanding what your competitors are doing well and where they fall short can reveal opportunities for differentiation and innovation.

Social media is a goldmine for understanding market needs. Platforms like Facebook, Twitter, Instagram, and LinkedIn host vibrant communities where potential customers discuss their preferences, frustrations, and desires. Use social listening tools like Hootsuite, Sprout Social, or Brandwatch to monitor conversations about your industry, track trending topics, and gather real-time feedback. Engaging with your audience on social media also allows you to build relationships and gain trust.

Another practical approach is to immerse yourself in the environment where your target customers spend their time. Attend industry events, trade shows, conferences, and community gatherings. These settings provide firsthand opportunities to observe behaviors, engage in conversations, and network with potential customers and industry experts. Pay attention to the problems they discuss and the solutions they seek.

Understanding market needs is not a one-time task but an ongoing process. Markets evolve, customer preferences change, and new trends emerge. Regularly updating your research ensures you stay relevant and responsive to these changes. Implement mechanisms for continuous feedback, such as customer satisfaction surveys, product reviews, and social media interactions. Use this feedback to refine your offerings and stay aligned with your customers' needs.

A case study that illustrates the importance of understanding market needs is Dropbox. When Dropbox was first launched, the founders realized that existing cloud storage solutions were either too complex or inadequate for average users. They conducted extensive market research to understand the needs of both tech-savvy users and everyday consumers. By addressing the need for a simple, reliable, and accessible cloud storage solution, Dropbox quickly gained traction and built a loyal customer base.

To effectively prioritize market needs, use techniques like the Kano Model. This model categorizes customer needs into basic needs, performance needs, and excitement needs. Basic needs are the must-haves that customers expect; performance needs are those that customers consciously desire and can improve satisfaction; excitement needs are unexpected features that can delight customers. By understanding and prioritizing these needs, you can allocate resources efficiently and enhance customer satisfaction.

Empathy mapping is another useful tool. This involves creating a visual representation of what customers say, think, feel, and do. It helps you step into your customers' shoes and gain a deeper emotional understanding of their experiences. Use empathy maps to guide product design, marketing messages, and customer service strategies.

Another aspect to consider is the Jobs-to-Be-Done framework, which focuses on understanding the underlying jobs that customers are trying to accomplish when they use a product or service. This framework shifts the perspective from what the customer is buying to why they are buying it. For example, a customer doesn't buy a drill because they want a drill; they buy it because they need to make a hole. By understanding the job your product is hired to do, you can innovate more effectively and meet your customers' needs more precisely.

Conducting Market Research

Market research is the backbone of any successful business strategy. It provides the insights you need to understand your audience, identify opportunities, minimize risks, and make informed decisions. Conducting effective market research involves a combination of methodologies and techniques to gather and analyze data about your target market, competitors, and overall industry landscape.

The journey begins with defining the objectives of your research. Are you looking to launch a new product, expand into a new market, or simply better understand your current customers? Clear objectives will guide your research process and help you focus on the most relevant information. For instance, if your goal is to understand customer satisfaction, you might focus on surveys and interviews that delve into user experiences and expectations.

Once your objectives are set, the next step is to choose the right research methods. Market research can be broadly categorized into primary and secondary research. Primary research involves collecting new data directly from sources, while secondary research relies on existing data.

Primary research is invaluable because it provides firsthand insights from your target audience. Surveys are one of the most common tools used in primary research. They can be distributed online, via email, or in person. When designing a survey, it's important to include a mix of question types: closed-ended questions for quantitative data and open-ended questions for qualitative insights. For example, you might ask customers to rate their satisfaction on a scale of 1 to 10 and then follow up with an open-ended question about how your product could be improved.

Interviews offer a more in-depth understanding of individual perspectives. Conducting one-on-one interviews allows you to explore specific issues in detail and ask follow-up questions based on the respondent's answers. Focus groups, on the other hand, provide a way to gather diverse opinions and observe group dynamics. In a focus group, a moderator guides a discussion among a small group of participants, encouraging them to share their thoughts and experiences.

Observational research is another powerful method, especially for understanding consumer behavior. By observing how people interact with products in natural settings, you can uncover insights that might not emerge from direct questioning. For example, if you're developing a new kitchen gadget, watching how people use similar tools in their homes can reveal practical challenges and preferences.

Secondary research involves analyzing existing data from various sources such as industry reports, academic journals, government publications, and market studies. This type of research is cost-effective and can provide a broad overview of market trends, competitive landscapes, and consumer behaviors. Organizations like Nielsen, Statista, and IBISWorld offer comprehensive reports that can be invaluable in this phase. Additionally, academic institutions and trade associations often publish research that can provide deeper insights into specific industries.

Competitive analysis is a critical component of market research. By studying your competitors, you can identify their strengths, weaknesses, and strategies. Start by listing your direct and indirect competitors, then analyze their products, pricing, marketing efforts, and customer reviews. Understanding what your competitors do well and where they fall short can help you position your own offerings more effectively. Tools like SWOT analysis (Strengths, Weaknesses, Opportunities, Threats) can provide a structured approach to this process.

Social media platforms are treasure troves of real-time consumer insights. By monitoring conversations on platforms like Twitter, Facebook, and Instagram, you can gain a sense of public sentiment about your industry, products, and competitors. Social listening tools such as Hootsuite or Brandwatch can automate this process, allowing you to track mentions, hashtags, and trends related to your business.

As you gather data, it's crucial to organize and analyze it systematically. Quantitative data from surveys and secondary sources can be analyzed using statistical methods to identify patterns and trends. Qualitative data from interviews and open-ended survey questions can be coded and categorized to highlight common themes and insights. Software tools like SPSS, NVivo, and Tableau can assist in this analysis, making it easier to visualize and interpret your findings.

One of the key challenges in market research is ensuring the reliability and validity of your data. To enhance reliability, use consistent methods and procedures throughout your research. For example, if you're conducting surveys, use the same questions and scales for all respondents. Validity, on the other hand, refers to the accuracy of your findings. To ensure validity, make sure your research questions are clearly defined and that your data collection methods are appropriate for your objectives.

Sampling is another critical consideration. The sample size and composition can significantly impact the accuracy and generalizability of your findings. Aim for a sample that is representative of your target market. For quantitative research, larger samples tend to yield more reliable results. For qualitative research, focus on achieving depth and diversity of insights rather than large numbers.

Analyzing your market research findings involves synthesizing the data to draw meaningful conclusions.

Look for patterns, trends, and correlations that can inform your business decisions. For instance, if you discover that a significant portion of your target market values sustainability, you might consider emphasizing eco-friendly features in your product design and marketing.

Once your analysis is complete, the next step is to present your findings in a clear and actionable format. Reports, presentations, and visualizations are effective ways to communicate your research results to stakeholders. Use charts, graphs, and infographics to highlight key data points and trends. Summarize the main insights and recommendations in an executive summary for quick reference. Ensure that your findings are actionable by linking them directly to your business objectives and suggesting specific strategies based on the data.

Analyzing Your Competition
Understanding your competition is crucial to the success of any business. Analyzing your competition involves more than just knowing who they are; it requires a deep dive into their strategies, strengths, weaknesses, and market positioning. This thorough analysis allows you to identify opportunities, differentiate your business, and craft strategies to gain a competitive edge.

The first step in analyzing your competition is identifying who your competitors are. Competitors can be categorized into direct and indirect competitors. Direct competitors offer the same or very similar products or services as you do. Indirect competitors provide different products or services that can satisfy the same customer need or solve the same problem. For instance, if you run a coffee shop, your direct competitors are other coffee shops, while indirect competitors might include cafes, fast food restaurants, and even convenience stores that sell coffee.

Once you have identified your competitors, gather as much information as possible about them. Start by examining their online presence. Visit their websites to understand their product offerings, pricing strategies, and unique selling propositions (USPs). Pay attention to their branding, messaging, and customer engagement tactics. Follow them on social media to see how they interact with their audience and the type of content they share.

Customer reviews and ratings on platforms like Yelp, Google Reviews, and social media can provide valuable insights into a competitor's strengths and weaknesses. Look for patterns in the feedback. Are customers consistently praising a particular aspect of their service? Are there recurring complaints? These insights can help you identify areas where your competitors excel and where they fall short, providing opportunities for you to differentiate your business.

Another effective way to gather information is by signing up for their newsletters and promotions. This gives you a firsthand look at how they communicate with their customers, the frequency and type of promotions they run, and any new products or services they are launching. Additionally, visiting their physical locations (if applicable) can offer insights into their customer service, store layout, and overall customer experience.

Competitor analysis tools can also be incredibly useful. Tools like SEMrush, Ahrefs, and SimilarWeb allow you to analyze competitors' online traffic, keywords, backlinks, and overall digital marketing strategies. These tools can show you where your competitors are getting their traffic from, which keywords they are ranking for, and how they are performing in search engine results. This information can help you identify gaps and opportunities in your own digital marketing efforts.

Benchmarking is a key component of competitive analysis. This involves comparing your business performance against your competitors on various metrics such as market share, sales volume, customer satisfaction, and social media engagement. Benchmarking helps you understand where you stand in the market relative to your competitors and identify areas for improvement.

A SWOT analysis (Strengths, Weaknesses, Opportunities, Threats) is a powerful tool for summarizing your findings. List your competitors' strengths and weaknesses based on the data you have gathered. Consider opportunities where you can capitalize on their weaknesses or gaps in the market that they are not addressing. Also, identify any threats they pose to your business, such as new product launches or aggressive marketing campaigns.

Understanding your competitors' business models and revenue streams is also important. How do they make money? Do they rely on a single product line, or do they have diversified offerings? Are they pursuing any innovative business models? For example, a competitor might offer a subscription service, freemium model, or bundled products. Understanding these aspects can provide insights into their strategies and help you identify potential opportunities for your own business.

Pricing strategies are a critical area of focus. Analyze how your competitors price their products or services. Are they using a cost-plus pricing strategy, value-based pricing, or competitive pricing? Understanding their pricing strategy can help you position your offerings accordingly. If a competitor is known for low prices, you might focus on differentiating through quality or added services. Conversely, if they are positioned as a premium brand, you might compete on affordability or convenience.

Promotional strategies are another key area to analyze. What types of promotions and discounts do your competitors offer? How often do they run these promotions? Are they leveraging seasonal trends or special events? Understanding their promotional tactics can help you plan your own marketing campaigns more effectively. For instance, if a competitor frequently offers discounts during holidays, you might consider running a loyalty program or exclusive offers to retain your customers during those times.

Customer loyalty programs can also provide insights. Analyze whether your competitors have loyalty programs, how they are structured, and what benefits they offer. Loyalty programs can be a significant differentiator, and understanding how competitors use them can inspire new ideas for your own customer retention strategies.

Innovation is another critical aspect to consider. Are your competitors investing in research and development? Are they launching new products or services regularly? Staying abreast of their innovations can help you anticipate market trends and ensure that your business remains competitive. For example, if a competitor is adopting new technologies or expanding into new markets, you might need to accelerate your own innovation efforts to keep pace.

One illustrative example of effective competitor analysis is the story of Nike and Adidas. Both companies are global leaders in the athletic footwear and apparel market, and their rivalry has been marked by keen competitive analysis and strategic responses. Nike, for instance, has consistently monitored Adidas's moves and market strategies. When Adidas began to gain traction with its retro-inspired designs and collaborations with celebrities and influencers, Nike responded by amplifying its own collaborations and focusing on innovative designs like the Flyknit and the React series. This constant monitoring and adjusting have allowed Nike to maintain its market leadership while pushing the boundaries of innovation and brand engagement.

Creating a Value Proposition

Crafting a compelling value proposition is a crucial element in building a successful business. It serves as the foundation for communicating the unique benefits your product or service offers to your target audience. A well-defined value proposition not only differentiates you from competitors but also connects emotionally with your customers, driving their decision to choose your brand over others.

To create an effective value proposition, start by understanding your target audience deeply. This involves identifying their needs, desires, and pain points. Conduct thorough market research, including surveys, interviews, and focus groups, to gather insights into what matters most to your potential customers. The more you know about their preferences and challenges, the better you can tailor your value proposition to resonate with them.

Once you have a clear understanding of your audience, focus on the unique benefits your product or service provides. These benefits should address the specific needs and pain points of your target customers. For example, if you are offering a time-saving software solution, highlight how it simplifies complex tasks and allows users to focus on more important aspects of their work. The key is to articulate how your product makes your customers' lives better or easier in a way that competitors do not.

A great value proposition is clear, concise, and compelling. It should be easy to understand and communicate the primary reason why a customer should choose your product or service. Avoid jargon and complex language that can confuse or alienate your audience. Instead, use straightforward language that speaks directly to the benefits your customers will experience.

Consider the example of Slack, a popular team collaboration tool. Slack's value proposition is succinct and powerful: "Be more productive at work with less effort." This statement clearly communicates the primary benefit of using Slack—enhanced productivity—while also implying ease of use. It addresses a common pain point (workplace productivity) and promises a solution in a concise manner.

Differentiation is another critical component of a strong value proposition. Identify what sets your product or service apart from the competition. This could be a unique feature, superior quality, exceptional customer service, or a combination of factors. Emphasize these differentiators in your value proposition to show why your offering is the best choice. For instance, if your product is made from sustainable materials, highlight this eco-friendly aspect to attract environmentally conscious consumers.

Storytelling can be a powerful tool in crafting your value proposition. People connect with stories on an emotional level, and a compelling narrative can make your proposition more memorable. Share the story behind your product or service, focusing on how it came to be and the problem it aims to solve. For example, if you started your business to address a personal frustration with existing solutions, share that journey with your audience. This not only humanizes your brand but also helps potential customers relate to your mission.

A successful value proposition also includes quantifiable benefits. Whenever possible, use specific numbers and data to back up your claims. For example, instead of saying your product "saves time," specify that it "reduces task completion time by 30%." Concrete data adds credibility to your value proposition and makes it more persuasive. If you have case studies, testimonials, or metrics from satisfied customers, incorporate these into your messaging to provide evidence of your product's effectiveness.

Testing and refining your value proposition is an ongoing process. Initially, brainstorm multiple versions and test them with your target audience through surveys, A/B testing, or focus groups. Gather feedback on what resonates most and make adjustments based on the insights you receive. This iterative approach ensures that your value proposition remains relevant and impactful as market conditions and customer preferences evolve.

One practical approach is to use the Value Proposition Canvas, a tool developed by Alexander Osterwalder. This framework helps you align your product or service with the specific needs and desires of your customers. The canvas consists of two main sections: the Customer Profile and the Value Map. The

Customer Profile details the jobs your customers need to get done, their pain points, and the gains they seek. The Value Map outlines the products and services you offer, how they relieve customer pains, and how they create gains. By matching these elements, you can craft a value proposition that is both customer-centric and clearly aligned with your offerings.

A compelling value proposition should be prominently featured across all your marketing channels. This includes your website, social media profiles, advertising campaigns, and sales materials. Consistency in messaging reinforces your value proposition and helps build brand recognition. Ensure that every touchpoint with your customers communicates the unique benefits of your product or service effectively.

Consider the success story of Apple and its value proposition for the iPhone. Apple's value proposition focuses on innovation, design, and user experience. By emphasizing these core benefits, Apple has built a loyal customer base that values the seamless integration of hardware and software, intuitive user interface, and cutting-edge technology. The consistent and compelling articulation of this value proposition across all marketing channels has solidified Apple's position as a leader in the smartphone market.

In addition to external communication, your value proposition should be embraced internally within your organization. Ensure that all team members understand and can articulate the unique benefits of your product or service. This internal alignment is essential for delivering a consistent customer experience that lives up to your value proposition. Training sessions, internal communications, and regular updates can help keep your team informed and motivated to uphold the brand promise.

Testing Your Idea with Minimum Viable Products (MVP)

Launching a new product or service can be a daunting endeavor, fraught with uncertainty and risk. One proven method to mitigate these challenges is by developing a Minimum Viable Product (MVP). An MVP is a simplified version of your product that includes just enough features to satisfy early adopters and provide feedback for future development. This approach allows you to test your idea in the real world, gather valuable insights, and make informed decisions about your product's direction without committing extensive resources upfront.

The first step in creating an MVP is to clearly define the problem you are trying to solve. Understanding your target audience's pain points is crucial. Conducting market research, including surveys, interviews, and competitor analysis, will help you identify the core issue your product aims to address. This foundational knowledge ensures that your MVP is designed to meet a genuine need, increasing the likelihood of its acceptance in the market.

Once you have a clear understanding of the problem, outline the key features that will form the core of your MVP. These features should directly address the primary pain points of your target audience. It's essential to resist the urge to include every possible feature in this initial version. Focus on what's absolutely necessary to solve the problem and deliver value to your users. Remember, the goal of an MVP is not to be a complete product but to test your assumptions and gather feedback with minimal investment.

Consider the example of Dropbox. Before developing the full product, the founders created a simple video demonstrating the core functionality of their cloud storage solution. This video served as their MVP, allowing them to gauge interest and collect feedback without building the actual product. The overwhelmingly positive response validated their idea and provided the confidence to proceed with development. This lean approach saved time and resources while ensuring they were on the right track.

Building an MVP often involves iterative design and development processes. Start with a prototype or a basic version of your product. This could be a landing page, a mock-up, or a simple interactive model. The key is to create something tangible that you can present to potential users. Use low-cost tools and technologies to develop this prototype, keeping expenses low and flexibility high.

Once your MVP is ready, it's time to test it with real users. Identify a group of early adopters who represent your target audience. These individuals should be willing to provide honest feedback and insights. Engaging with early adopters can be done through various channels, such as user testing sessions, beta programs, or crowdfunding campaigns. The feedback you gather from these initial users is invaluable. It will highlight what works, what doesn't, and what needs improvement.

During the testing phase, it's crucial to track key metrics that will inform your decision-making process. These metrics might include user engagement, retention rates, and conversion rates. Analyzing this data helps you understand how users interact with your product and identify any obstacles they face. For example, if users are abandoning the product after a few interactions, it might indicate usability issues or a mismatch between their expectations and the product's features.

The feedback loop created by testing your MVP should guide your development roadmap. Use the insights gained to prioritize feature enhancements and address any shortcomings. This iterative process allows you to build a product that better aligns with user needs and preferences. Each iteration brings you closer to a more refined and market-ready product.

Successful MVP testing also involves effective communication with your early adopters. Keep them informed about updates and improvements based on their feedback. This transparency fosters a sense of collaboration and loyalty, encouraging users to remain engaged and invested in your product's success. Moreover, early adopters can become advocates for your product, helping to spread the word and attract more users.

Consider the case of Airbnb. The company's initial MVP was a simple website that allowed the founders to rent out their own apartment to visitors. By testing this basic concept, they validated the demand for short-term, peer-to-peer lodging. The feedback from their first users helped them refine the platform, leading to the development of a successful global marketplace. Airbnb's journey illustrates how starting small and iterating based on real-world feedback can lead to significant growth and success.

Another critical aspect of MVP testing is maintaining flexibility and adaptability. Be prepared to pivot if the feedback indicates that your original assumptions were incorrect. Pivoting doesn't mean abandoning your vision; it means adjusting your approach to better meet market demands. For instance, Twitter started as a podcasting platform called Odeo. When the founders realized the potential of microblogging, they pivoted to create what we now know as Twitter. This shift was driven by the insights gained through initial user interactions and market feedback.

In addition to user feedback, pay attention to the competitive landscape. Analyze how your MVP compares to existing solutions in the market. Identify gaps that your product can fill and leverage these opportunities to differentiate yourself. Competitive analysis helps you refine your value proposition and position your product more effectively.

Moreover, consider the scalability of your MVP. As you gather feedback and make improvements, think about how your product can evolve to accommodate a larger user base and additional features. Scalability ensures that your product can grow seamlessly as demand increases. This forward-thinking approach helps avoid potential bottlenecks and technical debt that could impede future development.

Chapter 3: Crafting a Solid Business Plan

A well-crafted business plan is the cornerstone of any successful venture. It serves as a roadmap, guiding you through the various stages of business development, from inception to growth and beyond. Whether you're seeking investment, planning for future growth, or simply trying to organize your thoughts, a solid business plan is indispensable.

Start by clearly defining your business idea. This involves articulating what your business does, the products or services you offer, and the market need you aim to fill. This section, often referred to as the executive summary, should be concise yet compelling, providing a snapshot of your business that grabs the reader's attention. Think of it as your business's elevator pitch—succinct, engaging, and informative.

Next, delve into a detailed market analysis. Understanding your market is crucial for any business plan. Identify your target audience, their demographics, preferences, and behaviors. Conducting thorough market research will help you understand the landscape in which you'll be operating, including the competition. Analyze your competitors' strengths and weaknesses, and identify opportunities for differentiation. This analysis not only helps refine your business strategy but also demonstrates to potential investors that you have a deep understanding of the market.

Once you have a clear picture of the market, outline your business's organizational structure. Who are the key players in your organization? What roles will they fill, and what qualifications do they bring to the table? This section should include an overview of your management team, their responsibilities, and how their expertise will contribute to the business's success. For a small startup, this might be a brief overview, while a larger enterprise may require a more detailed hierarchy.

Detailing your product or service offering is the next crucial step. This section should describe what you are selling, how it benefits your customers, and what makes it unique. If you're developing a product, explain the lifecycle from development to launch, and any proprietary technology or patents that give you a competitive edge. For services, outline the process, key features, and customer benefits. Use clear, non-technical language to ensure that even readers without a background in your industry can understand your offering.

Marketing and sales strategies form the backbone of how you plan to attract and retain customers. Describe your marketing strategy in detail, including the channels you will use (online, offline, social media, etc.), your branding strategy, and any promotional activities. Explain how you will reach your target audience and convert them into paying customers. Additionally, outline your sales process, from lead generation to closing deals, and any after-sales support you will provide. This section should also include a discussion of your pricing strategy and how it compares to competitors.

No business plan is complete without a comprehensive financial plan. This should include detailed financial projections such as income statements, cash flow statements, and balance sheets for the next three to five years. Include assumptions behind your projections, such as expected revenue growth, cost estimates, and funding requirements. A break-even analysis is also valuable, showing when you expect your business to become profitable. Be realistic and conservative in your estimates to build credibility with potential investors.

Funding requirements and proposals are critical for businesses seeking investment. Clearly state how much funding you need, what it will be used for, and how it will help your business achieve its goals. Break down the funding requirements into specific categories such as marketing, product development, operations, and personnel. Also, outline your funding strategy—whether you're seeking debt financing, equity investment, or a combination of both, and the terms you're offering to investors.

Risk analysis and mitigation strategies are integral parts of a solid business plan. Identify potential risks that could impact your business, such as market fluctuations, regulatory changes, or operational challenges. Provide a realistic assessment of these risks and outline strategies for mitigating them. This shows investors that you are not only aware of potential pitfalls but also prepared to handle them.

To make your business plan engaging and easy to navigate, use a clear and professional format. Start with a cover page that includes your business name, logo, and contact information. Follow with a table of contents for easy reference. Each section should be clearly labeled, and the content should flow logically. Use charts, graphs, and tables to present data visually, making complex information more digestible.

Case studies and real-life examples can add significant value to your business plan. For instance, if you're launching a new tech product, include a case study of a similar product that successfully entered the market. Highlight lessons learned and how you plan to apply them to your business. This not only adds credibility but also shows that you've done your homework.

Consider the story of Spanx, the billion-dollar shapewear company founded by Sara Blakely. When Blakely started, she identified a clear market need for comfortable, effective shapewear. She conducted extensive market research, developed a prototype, and created a detailed business plan outlining her vision, market strategy, and financial projections. Her business plan helped secure initial funding and guided her through the early stages of growth. Today, Spanx is a global brand, a testament to the power of a well-crafted business plan.

After covering the essential sections of your business plan, it's crucial to include an implementation timeline. This timeline should outline key milestones and deliverables, providing a roadmap for how you will execute your plan. Include specific dates and deadlines for important tasks such as product development, market launch, and key hires. This helps keep your team on track and demonstrates to investors that you have a clear and actionable strategy.

Why a Business Plan is Essential

Launching a new business is an exhilarating endeavor, filled with visions of success and innovation. However, amidst the excitement, it's easy to overlook the critical foundation that can turn those dreams into reality: a meticulously crafted business plan. This document is not just a formality; it's the blueprint that will guide your business from conception through growth, helping you navigate the complexities of the entrepreneurial journey.

A business plan serves multiple crucial purposes, starting with providing clarity. When you're deep into the development of your idea, it's common to get lost in the details. A business plan forces you to step back and see the bigger picture. It requires you to outline your business objectives, the strategies you'll employ to achieve them, and the resources you'll need. This process of writing things down can reveal gaps in your thinking and areas that need more refinement, ensuring that your idea is as robust as possible before you dive in headfirst.

Consider the story of Howard Schultz, who transformed Starbucks from a small Seattle coffee bean retailer into a global coffeehouse chain. Schultz's vision for Starbucks was not just about selling coffee but creating a "third place" between work and home where people could relax and enjoy high-quality coffee. His business plan articulated this unique value proposition clearly, helping to secure the necessary investment and guiding the company's growth strategy. Today, Starbucks is a household name, with thousands of stores worldwide, thanks to the clarity and direction provided by a solid business plan.

Beyond providing clarity, a business plan is an essential tool for securing funding. Whether you're seeking venture capital, a bank loan, or even support from friends and family, potential investors need to see a well-thought-out plan that demonstrates the viability of your business. They want to know that you've done your homework, understand the market, and have a strategy for achieving profitability. A detailed business plan that includes market analysis, financial projections, and a clear path to growth can instill confidence in investors, increasing your chances of securing the necessary funds.

Moreover, a business plan acts as a roadmap, guiding you through each stage of your business's growth. It's easy to get sidetracked by day-to-day operations or unexpected challenges, but having a clear plan helps you stay focused on your long-term objectives. Your business plan should outline key milestones, such as product launches, market expansions, and revenue targets, and include timelines for achieving them. This roadmap not only keeps you on track but also makes it easier to measure your progress and adjust your strategy as needed.

Another critical aspect of a business plan is risk management. Every business faces uncertainties, from market fluctuations to operational challenges. A comprehensive business plan forces you to identify potential risks and develop strategies to mitigate them. This proactive approach to risk management can prevent small issues from becoming major problems and gives you a framework for responding to unforeseen events. For instance, during the early days of Airbnb, founders Brian Chesky and Joe Gebbia faced significant challenges in gaining user trust and managing regulatory hurdles. Their business plan included strategies for addressing these risks, such as implementing a robust review system and actively engaging with local governments, which helped them navigate these challenges and build a successful platform.

Furthermore, a business plan is indispensable for aligning your team. As your business grows, you'll need to bring on employees, partners, and other stakeholders. A clear, well-communicated business plan ensures that everyone understands the company's vision, objectives, and their role in achieving them. This alignment fosters a cohesive team culture and improves collaboration, as everyone is working towards the same goals. For example, when Elon Musk founded Tesla, his business plan not only outlined the company's mission to accelerate the world's transition to sustainable energy but also detailed the step-by-step strategy to achieve it. This clear vision attracted top talent and aligned the team's efforts, contributing to Tesla's rapid growth and success.

A business plan also plays a vital role in strategic planning and decision-making. As your business evolves, you'll face numerous decisions, from product development to market expansion. Your business plan provides a framework for evaluating these decisions, ensuring they align with your long-term objectives and available resources. This strategic approach helps you make informed choices that support sustainable growth and avoid the pitfalls of reactive decision-making.

Additionally, a business plan can enhance your business's credibility. In today's competitive market, credibility is crucial for building relationships with customers, suppliers, partners, and investors. A well-prepared business plan demonstrates professionalism and commitment, showing that you're serious about your business and have a clear strategy for success. This can open doors to new opportunities and partnerships that might otherwise be out of reach.

For instance, consider the case of Dropbox. Founder Drew Houston faced significant skepticism from investors when he first pitched his idea for a cloud-based file storage service. However, Houston's comprehensive business plan, which included detailed market analysis, technical feasibility, and a clear go-to-market strategy, helped convince investors of Dropbox's potential. This credibility was instrumental in securing initial funding, which enabled Dropbox to develop its product and achieve exponential growth.

Moreover, a business plan is a living document that evolves with your business. As market conditions change, new opportunities arise, or unforeseen challenges emerge, your business plan should be revisited and updated accordingly. This adaptability ensures that your business remains agile and responsive to the ever-changing business environment. By regularly reviewing and revising your plan, you can make informed adjustments to your strategy, keeping your business on the path to success.

Elements of a Strong Business Plan
A strong business plan is the cornerstone of a successful venture, serving as both a roadmap and a strategic tool for entrepreneurs. The elements of a well-crafted business plan not only provide clarity and direction but also play a crucial role in securing funding, guiding growth, and managing risks. Each component needs to be meticulously developed to ensure that the plan is comprehensive, coherent, and compelling.

The first element of a strong business plan is the executive summary. This section distills the essence of the entire plan into a concise, compelling overview. Although it appears at the beginning, the executive summary is typically written last, after all other sections are complete. It should include the business's mission statement, a brief description of products or services, the business's objectives, and a snapshot of financial projections. Consider it as your elevator pitch in written form. It must be engaging enough to capture the reader's attention and succinctly convey the value proposition.

The company description follows the executive summary. This section provides detailed information about the business, including its history, structure, and objectives. It should elaborate on what the business does, the market needs it addresses, and the unique selling proposition that sets it apart from competitors. This part of the plan should also outline the business's legal structure, ownership, and the qualifications of the management team. By providing a comprehensive background, the company description establishes a solid foundation for the rest of the business plan.

Market research and analysis are critical components that underpin the entire strategy. This section should offer a thorough analysis of the industry, market size, expected growth, target market segments, and competitive landscape. Understanding the market dynamics is essential for identifying opportunities and threats. Detailed customer profiles, including demographics, preferences, and buying behavior, help tailor marketing and operational strategies to meet market demands effectively. This section should also include a SWOT analysis (Strengths, Weaknesses, Opportunities, Threats) to provide a comprehensive view of the business's internal and external environment.

The organization and management section outlines the business's organizational structure. It should include an organizational chart that clearly defines the roles and responsibilities of key team members. Detailed biographies of the management team and board of directors, emphasizing their relevant experience and expertise, add credibility. This section should also address any gaps in the team and plans for addressing them. Investors are particularly interested in this part of the plan, as the strength of the management team often plays a pivotal role in the business's success.

Products or services offered by the business should be described in detail in their respective section. This part should explain what the business sells or what services it provides, emphasizing unique features and benefits. It should include information on the product lifecycle, research and development activities, and any intellectual property, such as patents or trademarks. If applicable, a description of future products or services in the pipeline can demonstrate long-term planning and growth potential. Highlighting the value proposition and how it meets customer needs better than existing solutions is crucial here.

The marketing and sales strategy section is where the plan outlines how the business intends to attract and retain customers. This should include a detailed marketing plan, covering aspects like pricing, promotion, distribution channels, and sales tactics. Market penetration strategies, advertising campaigns, and partnerships or alliances should be described. This section should also address the sales process, from lead generation to closing deals, and any customer service and retention strategies. A clear, actionable plan that aligns with market research findings shows that the business has a realistic approach to capturing and growing its market share.

Operational plans delve into the day-to-day functioning of the business. This section should describe the business's location, facilities, equipment, and technology requirements. It should also outline the production process, quality control measures, supply chain management, and inventory control. Understanding the logistics and operational workflow is essential for ensuring efficiency and scalability. If the business involves manufacturing, details on suppliers, production schedules, and contingency plans for disruptions should be included. This part of the plan provides a practical overview of how the business will deliver its products or services.

Financial projections are a critical component that potential investors scrutinize closely. This section should include detailed financial statements, such as income statements, cash flow statements, and balance sheets, typically for the next three to five years. Assumptions underlying these projections should be clearly stated and justified. Additionally, a break-even analysis, showing when the business expects to become profitable, is important. Financial projections should be realistic and based on sound data, reflecting both best-case and worst-case scenarios. This section should also include a funding request if the business is seeking external financing, outlining how much is needed, what it will be used for, and proposed terms.

An appendix at the end of the business plan can provide supplementary information that supports the main sections. This might include resumes of key team members, technical specifications, market research data, legal documents, and any other relevant material. The appendix should be well-organized and referenced in the main sections of the plan where appropriate. Including this additional information can reinforce the credibility and thoroughness of the business plan.

Crafting each of these elements with care and precision ensures that the business plan is not only comprehensive but also compelling to potential stakeholders. Each section should flow logically into the next, creating a narrative that clearly articulates the business's vision and strategy. The aim is to leave no doubt in the reader's mind about the potential for success and the meticulous planning that has gone into preparing for it.

Setting Realistic Goals and Milestones
Setting realistic goals and milestones is a fundamental aspect of successful business planning and execution. Goals provide direction and purpose, while milestones offer checkpoints that help measure progress and maintain momentum. For entrepreneurs and business owners, mastering the art of setting achievable goals and defining clear milestones can significantly enhance the likelihood of long-term success.

Understanding the importance of setting realistic goals begins with defining what constitutes a "realistic" goal. A realistic goal is one that is attainable given the current resources, time frame, and market conditions. Setting overly ambitious goals can lead to frustration and burnout, while goals that are too modest may not challenge you enough to push the business forward. The key is to find a balance that stretches your capabilities without setting you up for failure.

The SMART criteria—Specific, Measurable, Achievable, Relevant, and Time-bound—are widely recognized as an effective framework for goal setting. Specific goals are clear and unambiguous, leaving no room for misinterpretation. For instance, instead of setting a goal to "increase sales," a more specific goal would be to "increase sales by 20% within the next six months." Measurability ensures that you can track progress and determine when the goal has been achieved. Achievability is crucial; the goal should be challenging yet attainable with the resources at hand. Relevance ensures that the goal aligns with broader business objectives, and being time-bound adds a sense of urgency and helps prioritize tasks.

Once goals are established, breaking them down into smaller, manageable milestones is essential. Milestones act as stepping stones, providing clear points of reference along the journey. They make large, daunting goals more approachable and allow for incremental achievements that build confidence and maintain motivation. For example, if the goal is to launch a new product within a year, milestones might include completing market research in the first quarter, finalizing product design in the second quarter, beginning production in the third quarter, and launching the product in the fourth quarter.

Effective goal setting also requires a thorough understanding of your business environment and capabilities. This involves conducting a SWOT analysis—identifying strengths, weaknesses, opportunities, and threats. By understanding these factors, you can set goals that leverage your strengths, address weaknesses, exploit opportunities, and mitigate threats. For example, if a strength is a strong online presence, a relevant goal might be to increase online sales through targeted digital marketing campaigns.

Involving your team in the goal-setting process can enhance buy-in and commitment. When team members participate in setting goals, they are more likely to understand the rationale behind them and feel a sense of ownership. This collaborative approach can also bring diverse perspectives and ideas, making the goals more robust and achievable. Regular team meetings to discuss progress, address challenges, and celebrate milestones can foster a positive and motivated work environment.

Flexibility is another critical component of realistic goal setting. Business environments are often unpredictable, and rigid goals can become irrelevant or unattainable in the face of changing circumstances. Being open to reassessment and adjustment of goals ensures that they remain relevant and attainable. For instance, if market conditions change unexpectedly, it might be necessary to revise sales targets or shift focus to new opportunities.

Tracking progress towards goals and milestones is vital for maintaining momentum and making informed decisions. Regularly reviewing performance against set targets helps identify areas where adjustments might be needed. This can be done through key performance indicators (KPIs), which provide quantifiable measures of success. For example, if a goal is to improve customer satisfaction, a relevant KPI might be the Net Promoter Score (NPS). Monitoring KPIs allows for timely interventions and helps keep the team focused on what matters most.

Celebrating achievements is an often-overlooked aspect of goal setting. Recognizing and rewarding progress, no matter how small, can boost morale and reinforce a culture of success. Whether it's a team lunch, a shout-out in a meeting, or a formal recognition program, celebrating milestones can motivate the team and build a positive work environment. It's important to acknowledge the hard work and dedication that go into achieving goals, fostering a sense of accomplishment and pride.

Setting realistic goals and milestones also involves a degree of self-awareness and personal discipline. Entrepreneurs and business leaders must be honest about their capabilities and limitations and be willing to seek help when needed. This might mean hiring a consultant, investing in training, or simply asking for advice from mentors and peers. Self-discipline is crucial for staying focused on goals, avoiding distractions, and maintaining the perseverance needed to overcome obstacles.

Long-term goals are equally important as short-term ones. While short-term goals provide immediate direction and motivation, long-term goals give a sense of purpose and vision. They help align daily activities with the broader mission of the business, ensuring that short-term efforts contribute to long-term success. For example, a long-term goal might be to become the market leader in your industry, while short-term goals might include increasing market share, improving product quality, and expanding distribution channels.

Risk management is another essential aspect of setting realistic goals. Identifying potential risks and developing mitigation strategies ensures that you are prepared for uncertainties. For example , if you're planning to expand into a new market, it's essential to consider economic fluctuations, regulatory changes, and competitive actions that could impact your plans. Developing contingency plans for these scenarios can help maintain progress towards your goals even when faced with unexpected challenges.

Developing Financial Projections
Financial projections are a crucial component of any business plan. They serve as a roadmap for the future, offering a detailed view of the financial health and potential growth of a business. For beginners, developing financial projections may seem daunting, but with a clear understanding of the fundamental components and a methodical approach, it becomes a manageable and enlightening process.

The first step in developing financial projections is understanding the basic elements involved. These typically include revenue forecasts, expense estimates, cash flow projections, and profit and loss statements. Each of these elements provides different insights into the business's financial performance and helps in making informed decisions.

Revenue forecasts are the cornerstone of financial projections. They estimate the amount of money your business will generate over a specific period, usually broken down into monthly or quarterly increments. To create accurate revenue forecasts, start by analyzing historical sales data if available. Look at trends, seasonality, and any factors that have influenced sales in the past. For new businesses without historical data, market research is essential. Identify your target market, understand your competition, and estimate how much of the market you can realistically capture. Consider different scenarios – best-case, worst-case, and most likely – to cover a range of possibilities.

Once revenue forecasts are established, the next step is to estimate expenses. Expenses can be categorized into fixed and variable costs. Fixed costs are those that remain constant regardless of the business's performance, such as rent, salaries, and insurance. Variable costs fluctuate with the level of production or sales, including raw materials, shipping, and commissions. It's important to be thorough and realistic when estimating expenses. Overlooking small costs can lead to significant discrepancies in your projections. Review your business operations in detail, consult with suppliers, and research industry standards to ensure your estimates are comprehensive.

Cash flow projections are another vital aspect of financial planning. Cash flow is the movement of money in and out of your business, and it's crucial for ensuring you have enough liquidity to meet your obligations. Positive cash flow means more money is coming in than going out, allowing you to reinvest in your business, pay off debts, and save for future needs. Negative cash flow, on the other hand, can lead to financial strain and even bankruptcy if not managed properly. To create cash flow projections, start with your revenue forecasts and subtract your estimated expenses. Include other cash inflows and outflows, such as loans, investments, and tax payments. Regularly updating your cash flow projections helps you stay on top of your financial situation and make necessary adjustments.

The profit and loss statement, or income statement, summarizes the revenues, costs, and expenses incurred during a specific period. It shows whether the business is profitable or not by calculating the net profit (or loss) after all expenses are deducted from total revenue. This statement provides a snapshot of the business's financial performance and is essential for investors and lenders. To develop a profit and loss statement, compile your revenue forecasts and expense estimates. Subtract the total expenses from the total revenue to determine your net profit. Regularly reviewing your profit and loss statement helps identify trends and areas for improvement.

Developing financial projections also involves creating balance sheets. A balance sheet provides a snapshot of your business's financial position at a specific point in time, detailing assets, liabilities, and equity. Assets include everything the business owns, such as cash, inventory, and property. Liabilities are obligations the business owes, like loans and accounts payable. Equity represents the owner's investment in the business. To create a balance sheet, list all assets and their values, followed by liabilities and their amounts. The difference between assets and liabilities gives you the equity. A healthy balance sheet shows more assets than liabilities, indicating a strong financial position.

To ensure the accuracy and reliability of your financial projections, it's important to use consistent and realistic assumptions. Assumptions are the underlying factors that influence your projections, such as sales growth rates, cost inflation, and market conditions. Being overly optimistic with your assumptions can lead to unrealistic projections and potential financial difficulties. On the other hand, being too conservative might undervalue your business's potential. Research industry benchmarks, consult with experts, and base your assumptions on realistic and achievable figures.

Another critical aspect of developing financial projections is sensitivity analysis. Sensitivity analysis examines how changes in key assumptions impact your financial projections. By adjusting variables such as sales volume, pricing, and cost of goods sold, you can see how sensitive your projections are to changes and identify potential risks. This analysis helps you prepare for different scenarios and develop contingency plans. For example, if your projections are highly sensitive to changes in sales volume, you might focus on strategies to boost marketing efforts or diversify your product offerings.

Incorporating a break-even analysis into your financial projections is also beneficial. A break-even analysis determines the point at which your business covers all its costs and starts to make a profit. This analysis helps you understand the minimum sales needed to avoid losses and informs pricing and cost management strategies. To conduct a break-even analysis, calculate your fixed and variable costs, and determine the price at which you will sell your products or services. The break-even point is found by dividing the total fixed costs by the difference between the unit price and the variable cost per unit. This calculation provides a clear target for your sales efforts and can guide decisions related to pricing and cost control.

Creating an Execution Roadmap

An execution roadmap is a strategic plan that outlines the steps necessary to achieve your business goals. It serves as a detailed guide, breaking down long-term objectives into manageable tasks and timelines. For beginners, creating an execution roadmap can seem overwhelming, but with a structured approach, it becomes a powerful tool for driving progress and ensuring accountability.

The first step in creating an execution roadmap is to clearly define your business goals. These goals should be specific, measurable, achievable, relevant, and time-bound (SMART). For example, instead of setting a vague goal like "increase sales," aim for "increase sales by 20% within the next year." This specificity provides a concrete target and a timeframe, making it easier to plan the necessary steps.

Once your goals are defined, the next step is to break them down into smaller, actionable tasks. This process, known as task decomposition, involves identifying all the activities required to achieve each goal. For instance, if your goal is to increase sales, tasks might include market research, developing a marketing campaign, training the sales team, and optimizing your sales funnel. Each of these tasks can be further broken down into sub-tasks, creating a comprehensive list of actions that need to be taken.

A crucial aspect of task decomposition is prioritization. Not all tasks are of equal importance or urgency. Prioritizing tasks ensures that the most critical activities are addressed first, allowing for more efficient use of resources and time. One effective method for prioritizing tasks is the Eisenhower Matrix, which categorizes tasks into four quadrants based on their urgency and importance. This helps you focus on what truly matters and avoid getting sidetracked by less critical activities.

With your tasks prioritized, the next step is to assign responsibilities. Clearly defining who is responsible for each task ensures accountability and prevents overlap or confusion. When assigning responsibilities, consider the strengths and expertise of your team members. Aligning tasks with individual skills not only enhances efficiency but also increases the likelihood of successful outcomes. In addition, providing clear instructions and expectations helps team members understand their roles and responsibilities, fostering a sense of ownership and commitment.

Creating a timeline is another essential component of an execution roadmap. Timelines provide a visual representation of when tasks need to be completed and help track progress. Begin by setting deadlines for each task and sub-task, ensuring they are realistic and achievable. Gantt charts are a popular tool for visualizing timelines, as they show the start and end dates of tasks, their duration, and any dependencies between tasks. Regularly updating your timeline and adjusting deadlines as needed keeps your roadmap flexible and responsive to changes.

Resource allocation is a critical consideration when developing an execution roadmap. Resources include time, money, personnel, and materials. Ensuring that you have adequate resources to complete each task is vital for success. This may involve budgeting, scheduling, and securing additional resources if necessary. For example, if a marketing campaign requires a significant budget, you may need to allocate funds from other areas or seek external financing. Similarly, if a task requires specialized skills, you may need to hire additional staff or provide training for existing employees.

Communication is key to the successful implementation of an execution roadmap. Regular updates and open channels of communication keep everyone informed and aligned with the overall plan. Holding regular meetings to review progress, address challenges, and make adjustments as needed fosters a collaborative environment and ensures that everyone is working towards the same goals. Transparent communication also helps in identifying potential issues early, allowing for timely interventions and solutions.

Monitoring and evaluation are ongoing processes that are integral to an effective execution roadmap. Regularly tracking progress against your timeline and goals allows you to measure success and identify areas for improvement. Key performance indicators (KPIs) are useful metrics for evaluating progress. For example, if your goal is to increase sales, relevant KPIs might include monthly sales figures, conversion rates, and customer acquisition costs. Analyzing these metrics provides insights into what is working and what needs adjustment.

Flexibility is an important attribute of a successful execution roadmap. Business environments are dynamic, and unexpected challenges or opportunities can arise. Being able to adapt your roadmap in response to these changes is crucial. This might involve revising timelines, reallocating resources, or adjusting goals. Maintaining flexibility ensures that your roadmap remains relevant and effective, even in the face of uncertainty.

Celebrating milestones and successes is an often overlooked but important aspect of an execution roadmap. Recognizing and rewarding achievements boosts morale and motivation, reinforcing the importance of the work being done. Whether it's a team lunch, a shout-out in a meeting, or a formal recognition program, celebrating successes fosters a positive work environment and encourages continued effort and commitment.

A well-crafted execution roadmap also includes contingency planning. Contingency plans are backup strategies that address potential risks and challenges. Identifying possible obstacles and developing plans to mitigate them ensures that you are prepared for unforeseen events. For example, if a key supplier fails to deliver on time, having an alternative supplier lined up can prevent delays. Contingency planning reduces uncertainty and provides a safety net, allowing for smoother execution of your roadmap.

Technology can be a valuable ally in creating and managing your execution roadmap. Various project management tools and software solutions are available to streamline the planning, tracking, and communication processes. Tools like Trello, Asana, and Microsoft Project offer features such as task assignment, deadline tracking, progress visualization, and team collaboration. These tools can help you stay organized, ensure that nothing falls through the cracks, and facilitate real-time updates and adjustments.

Chapter 4: Securing Funding

Securing funding is a critical step in turning your business idea into a reality. Whether you're starting a new venture or looking to expand an existing one, having sufficient capital is essential for growth. However, the process of obtaining funds can be complex and daunting, especially for beginners. This chapter provides practical advice and actionable steps to help you navigate this journey successfully.

Understanding your funding needs is the first step. Before approaching potential investors or lenders, you need a clear picture of how much money you require and how it will be used. Create a detailed business plan outlining your financial needs, including startup costs, operational expenses, marketing budgets, and contingency funds. This plan should also include financial projections, such as income statements, cash flow forecasts, and balance sheets. Having a comprehensive understanding of your financial needs not only helps in securing funding but also demonstrates to potential investors that you are well-prepared and serious about your venture.

There are various sources of funding available, each with its own advantages and disadvantages. Personal savings and contributions from friends and family are often the first avenues entrepreneurs explore. While these sources can be relatively easy to access, it's important to treat them with the same level of professionalism as any other funding source. Clearly outline the terms of the investment or loan, including repayment schedules and equity stakes, to avoid potential misunderstandings or conflicts.

Equity financing is a popular option, particularly for startups. This involves selling a portion of your business to investors in exchange for capital. Angel investors and venture capitalists are common sources of equity financing. Angel investors are typically high-net-worth individuals who provide early-stage funding, often in exchange for an equity stake and some level of involvement in the business. Venture capitalists, on the other hand, are professional investors who manage pooled funds from various sources and invest in high-potential companies. While equity financing can provide significant capital, it also means giving up a portion of ownership and control.

Debt financing is another viable option. This involves borrowing money that must be repaid with interest. Traditional bank loans, lines of credit, and small business loans are common forms of debt financing. To secure a loan, you will typically need to provide collateral and demonstrate your ability to repay the debt through a solid business plan and financial projections. While debt financing allows you to retain full ownership of your business, it also brings the obligation of regular repayments, which can be a burden, especially for new businesses with uncertain cash flows.

Crowdfunding has emerged as an innovative and increasingly popular method of raising funds. Platforms like Kickstarter, Indiegogo, and GoFundMe allow entrepreneurs to present their business ideas to a large audience and raise small amounts of money from many people. Crowdfunding can be particularly effective for consumer-facing products or services with a compelling story or unique proposition. In addition to raising funds, crowdfunding can also serve as a marketing tool, helping to build a customer base and generate buzz around your business.

Grants and competitions are another avenue worth exploring. Various government agencies, non-profit organizations, and private entities offer grants and hold competitions to support innovative business ideas. Unlike loans, grants do not need to be repaid, making them an attractive source of funding. However, the application process can be highly competitive and time-consuming. Thorough research is required to identify relevant opportunities and tailor your application to meet the specific criteria.

Once you have identified potential funding sources, the next step is to prepare and present a compelling case to potential investors or lenders. Your business plan plays a crucial role in this process. It should be clear, concise, and persuasive, highlighting the uniqueness of your business idea, the market opportunity, your business model, and your financial projections. Additionally, a well-crafted pitch deck can be an effective tool for presenting your case. The pitch deck should include key elements such as your value proposition, market analysis, business model, competitive landscape, financial projections, and the amount of funding you are seeking.

Building relationships with potential investors is key to securing funding. Networking events, industry conferences, and startup incubators or accelerators can provide valuable opportunities to connect with investors. Building a rapport and establishing trust with potential investors can significantly increase your chances of securing funding. Be prepared to articulate your vision, demonstrate your knowledge of the market, and show your commitment to your business.

During the funding process, due diligence is a crucial step. Investors and lenders will conduct thorough investigations into your business to assess its viability and potential risks. This process can include reviewing your financial statements, business plan, market analysis, and legal documents. Being transparent and well-prepared for due diligence demonstrates your professionalism and can expedite the funding process.

Negotiating the terms of the funding is another important aspect. Whether you are dealing with equity investors or lenders, it is essential to understand the terms being offered and how they will impact your business. Key terms to consider include the interest rate, repayment schedule, equity stake, valuation, and any covenants or conditions. It may be beneficial to seek advice from a financial advisor or legal professional to ensure that the terms are fair and align with your long-term business goals.

After securing funding, effective management of the capital is critical to ensure that it is used efficiently and drives the intended business growth. Setting up a robust financial management system helps in tracking expenses, monitoring cash flow, and ensuring that funds are allocated appropriately. Regular financial reporting and analysis can provide insights into the performance of your business and highlight areas where adjustments may be necessary.

Bootstrapping Your Business

Bootstrapping your business is a path many entrepreneurs take when they want to maintain control and independence while avoiding the complexities of external funding. This approach involves using personal savings, reinvesting profits, and leveraging creativity and resourcefulness to grow the business. While it requires discipline and strategic planning, bootstrapping can lead to a more resilient and sustainable venture.

Starting with minimal resources necessitates a lean mindset. Every dollar counts, and spending must be meticulously planned and justified. Begin by clearly defining your business vision and objectives. A focused vision helps you prioritize expenditures and avoid unnecessary costs. For instance, instead of renting an expensive office space, consider working from home or using a co-working space. Utilize free or low-cost tools and software for essential business functions such as accounting, marketing, and project management.

One of the keys to successful bootstrapping is to start small and scale gradually. Begin by offering a minimum viable product (MVP) that addresses a specific market need. An MVP allows you to test your concept with minimal investment, gather feedback, and make necessary adjustments. This iterative approach reduces the risk of large-scale failures and ensures that your product or service meets customer demands. By focusing on core features, you can attract early adopters and generate initial revenue, which can be reinvested into the business.

Maximizing cash flow is crucial when bootstrapping. Aim to achieve positive cash flow as quickly as possible by minimizing expenses and accelerating revenue generation. Negotiate favorable payment terms with suppliers and incentivize customers to pay upfront or quickly. Implementing a subscription model or offering pre-orders can provide immediate cash inflows. Additionally, closely monitor your receivables and follow up promptly on overdue invoices to maintain liquidity.

Marketing on a tight budget requires ingenuity. Leverage the power of digital marketing, which can be highly cost-effective. Social media platforms offer a free or low-cost way to reach your target audience and build a community around your brand. Content marketing, such as blogging, video tutorials, and webinars, can establish your expertise and attract potential customers. Collaborate with influencers or other businesses for cross-promotions, which can expand your reach without significant expenditure. Email marketing remains a powerful tool for nurturing leads and maintaining customer relationships.

Networking is another powerful strategy for bootstrapped businesses. Building a strong network can open doors to valuable resources, advice, and opportunities. Attend industry events, join professional associations, and participate in online forums relevant to your field. Engage with mentors and peers who can offer guidance and support. These relationships can lead to partnerships, referrals, and collaborations that benefit your business. Moreover, networking helps you stay informed about industry trends and best practices.

Efficiency and productivity are critical when resources are limited. Streamline your operations by automating repetitive tasks and optimizing workflows. Invest time in learning and implementing productivity tools such as customer relationship management (CRM) systems, project management software, and communication platforms. Delegate tasks that are outside your expertise or that consume too much time, but do so judiciously to ensure cost-effectiveness. Hiring freelancers or part-time employees can be a flexible and economical way to expand your team without committing to full-time salaries.

Customer feedback is invaluable for a bootstrapped business. Engage with your customers regularly to understand their needs, preferences, and pain points. Use surveys, interviews, and social media interactions to gather insights. Act on this feedback to improve your offerings and enhance customer satisfaction. Happy customers are more likely to become repeat buyers and advocates for your brand, providing free word-of-mouth marketing.

Managing finances prudently is paramount. Maintain detailed financial records and regularly review your budget to track income and expenses. Identify areas where you can cut costs without compromising quality. For example, negotiate better rates with suppliers, reduce energy consumption, or find more affordable marketing channels. Keep a close eye on your cash flow and set aside an emergency fund to cushion against unexpected expenses or downturns.

Reinvesting profits is a cornerstone of bootstrapping. Instead of drawing large salaries or distributing profits, reinvest earnings back into the business to fuel growth. This could mean upgrading equipment, expanding your product line, increasing marketing efforts, or hiring additional staff. Reinvestment accelerates business development and positions you for long-term success.

Maintaining a strong company culture is vital, even in the early stages. A positive and supportive work environment boosts morale, productivity, and loyalty. Foster open communication, recognize achievements, and provide opportunities for professional growth. A motivated team is more likely to go above and beyond to help your business succeed. Additionally, a strong culture can attract top talent, even when you can't offer the highest salaries.

Bootstrapping also means being prepared for challenges and setbacks. Resilience and adaptability are essential traits for an entrepreneur. View obstacles as opportunities to learn and innovate. Maintain a problem-solving mindset and be willing to pivot or adjust your strategies as needed. Surround yourself with a supportive network of friends, family, and mentors who can provide encouragement and advice during tough times.

Long-term planning is crucial for sustained success. While short-term goals are important, keep an eye on the future.

Develop a strategic plan that outlines your vision for the next five to ten years. This plan should include key milestones, growth targets, and the steps necessary to achieve them. Regularly review and update your plan to reflect changes in the market, new opportunities, and lessons learned from your experiences.

Approaching Angel Investors and Venture Capitalists

Securing investment from angel investors and venture capitalists (VCs) can be a transformative step for your startup, providing not only the financial resources needed for growth but also valuable mentorship and industry connections. However, approaching these investors requires thorough preparation, strategic planning, and a compelling pitch that clearly communicates the potential of your business. This chapter will guide you through the critical steps and best practices to effectively engage with angel investors and VCs.

Begin by understanding the differences between angel investors and venture capitalists. Angel investors are typically high-net-worth individuals who invest their own money into startups, often in the early stages. They can be more flexible and willing to take on higher risks compared to VCs. On the other hand, venture capitalists manage pooled funds from various investors, including institutions, and tend to invest larger sums in companies with proven traction and growth potential. Knowing these distinctions will help you tailor your approach and pitch accordingly.

Before reaching out to potential investors, ensure your business is investment-ready. This means having a solid business plan, a clear value proposition, a scalable business model, and a capable team. Investors look for startups with a strong foundation and a realistic path to growth. Demonstrating traction, such as customer acquisition, revenue growth, or strategic partnerships, can significantly enhance your appeal. Conduct a thorough assessment of your business to identify any gaps or weaknesses that need to be addressed before seeking investment.

Crafting a compelling pitch is crucial. Your pitch should succinctly convey your business idea, market opportunity, competitive landscape, business model, and growth strategy. Start with a powerful elevator pitch that captures the essence of your business in a few sentences. Follow this with a detailed presentation that includes market analysis, product or service differentiation, financial projections, and an overview of your team's expertise. Highlight the problem you are solving and how your solution is uniquely positioned to address it. Use data and evidence to support your claims, and be prepared to answer tough questions about your business.

Building relationships with potential investors is as important as the pitch itself. Networking plays a crucial role in finding the right investors who align with your business vision and values. Attend industry conferences, startup events, and networking meetups to connect with investors and other entrepreneurs. Leverage online platforms like LinkedIn and AngelList to identify and reach out to potential investors. Personal introductions from mutual contacts can also be very effective. Building a rapport with investors before formally pitching to them can increase your chances of securing funding.

When approaching angel investors, it's beneficial to understand their individual investment preferences and motivations. Some angels invest for the potential financial returns, while others may be more interested in supporting innovative ideas or passionate entrepreneurs. Research your prospective angel investors to understand their previous investments and areas of interest. Tailor your pitch to align with their investment criteria and demonstrate how your business fits into their portfolio.

Venture capitalists, on the other hand, often have more structured investment processes and criteria. They typically look for startups with high growth potential, large addressable markets, and competitive advantages. When approaching VCs, it's essential to target the right firms based on their investment stage, sector focus, and geographic preference. Study the portfolios of different VC firms to identify those that have invested in companies similar to yours. This alignment increases the likelihood that they will be interested in your startup.

Securing a meeting with angel investors or VCs requires a well-crafted and concise email or message. Your initial outreach should include a brief introduction, an overview of your business, and a clear value proposition. Highlight any notable achievements or traction to capture their interest. Avoid sending lengthy business plans or detailed financials in the initial email; instead, focus on sparking their curiosity and securing a meeting where you can present your full pitch.

During the pitch meeting, focus on storytelling and building a narrative around your business. Investors want to understand not just the facts and figures but also the vision and passion behind your startup. Start with a compelling story about how you identified the problem and developed your solution. Use visuals and real-life examples to illustrate your points. Be confident, but also be prepared to listen and engage in a dialogue. Investors may ask challenging questions to test your understanding and commitment. Answering these questions thoughtfully and honestly can build credibility and trust.

Negotiating the terms of investment is a critical step once an investor shows interest. Understand the key terms commonly included in investment deals, such as valuation, equity stake, liquidation preferences, and board composition. It's advisable to seek legal counsel to help you navigate these negotiations and protect your interests. Aim for a fair deal that aligns the incentives of both parties and sets a solid foundation for a long-term partnership.

After securing investment, maintaining regular communication with your investors is essential. Keep them informed about your progress, challenges, and milestones. Regular updates build trust and demonstrate your commitment to transparency. Investors can provide valuable guidance, introductions, and resources, so actively seek their input and leverage their expertise. A strong relationship with your investors can be a significant asset as you navigate the ups and downs of growing your business.

One common mistake entrepreneurs make is approaching investors too early, before their business is ready for external funding. Prematurely seeking investment can lead to rejection and potentially damage your reputation in the investment community. Ensure you have a validated product, initial traction, and a clear path to growth before reaching out. Taking the time to build a solid foundation will not only increase your chances of securing investment but also put you in a stronger negotiating position.

Applying for Small Business Loans
Securing a small business loan can be a pivotal step in the growth and sustainability of your enterprise. Whether you're looking to expand operations, purchase inventory, invest in new equipment, or simply manage cash flow, a well-structured loan can provide the necessary capital to drive your business forward. However, the process of applying for a small business loan can be intricate and demanding. This chapter will guide you through the essential steps and best practices to enhance your chances of obtaining a loan that suits your business needs.

First and foremost, it's crucial to understand your financing requirements and the type of loan that best fits those needs. Small business loans come in various forms, including term loans, lines of credit, equipment financing, and SBA (Small Business Administration) loans. Each type of loan has its advantages and specific use cases. For instance, term loans are ideal for significant one-time investments, while lines of credit can help manage short-term working capital needs. Before approaching lenders, clearly define the purpose of the loan and the amount of capital you require. This clarity will not only streamline your application process but also demonstrate to lenders that you have a well-thought-out plan for the funds.

A critical aspect of your loan application is your business plan. Lenders need to see a comprehensive and realistic business plan that outlines your business model, market analysis, competitive landscape, marketing strategy, and financial projections. Your business plan should convey a deep understanding of your industry and how your business intends to succeed within it. Highlighting your unique value proposition and the steps you will take to achieve your goals will help build confidence with potential lenders. Ensure that your financial projections are detailed and realistic, reflecting both optimistic and conservative scenarios. This transparency will show lenders that you have considered various outcomes and have plans in place to manage potential risks.

Your personal and business credit scores play a significant role in the loan approval process. Lenders use these scores to assess your creditworthiness and determine the level of risk involved in lending to you. Before applying for a loan, review your credit reports from major credit bureaus and address any discrepancies or negative marks. Improving your credit score, if necessary, can take time, so start this process well in advance. For business credit, make sure that all your business accounts are in good standing, and consider establishing or strengthening relationships with vendors and creditors who report positive payment history to credit bureaus.

Collateral can be an important consideration for many lenders, especially for larger loans. Collateral refers to assets that you pledge to secure the loan, such as real estate, equipment, or inventory. If you default on the loan, the lender can seize the collateral to recover their losses. While not all loans require collateral, offering it can improve your chances of approval and potentially lower the interest rate. Carefully evaluate what assets you can use as collateral and understand the risks involved. It's crucial to balance the benefits of securing the loan with the potential consequences if your business faces financial difficulties.

Another key element of your loan application is your financial documentation. Lenders will request detailed financial statements, including income statements, balance sheets, and cash flow statements. These documents provide a snapshot of your business's financial health and performance. Ensure that your financial records are accurate, up-to-date, and professionally prepared. Lenders will also look at your tax returns, both personal and business, to assess your overall financial stability. Having thorough and organized financial documentation not only speeds up the application process but also builds credibility with lenders.

When you're ready to apply for a loan, research potential lenders to find those that best match your business needs and profile. Banks, credit unions, online lenders, and alternative financing companies each have different criteria and loan products. Traditional banks might offer lower interest rates but have more stringent requirements, while online lenders may provide faster approval with higher rates. The SBA also partners with various lenders to offer loans with favorable terms for small businesses. By understanding the strengths and weaknesses of different lenders, you can target your application to those most likely to approve your loan.

Crafting a compelling loan application involves more than just filling out forms and submitting documents. It's about telling the story of your business and demonstrating why it is a good investment. Write a strong cover letter that introduces your business, explains the purpose of the loan, and highlights key aspects of your business plan and financial health. Be honest about any challenges your business has faced and how you have addressed them. Authenticity and transparency can build trust with lenders and set you apart from other applicants.

Once you submit your loan application, be prepared for a thorough review process. Lenders will conduct due diligence to verify the information provided and assess the risk of lending to your business. This process may involve follow-up questions, requests for additional documentation, and interviews. Respond promptly and comprehensively to any inquiries from the lender. Demonstrating professionalism and responsiveness can positively influence the lender's perception of your business.

If your loan application is approved, carefully review the terms and conditions before accepting the offer. Pay close attention to the interest rate, repayment schedule, fees, and any covenants or restrictions. Understanding these terms is crucial to managing your loan effectively and avoiding any surprises down the line. If there are any terms that you do not understand or that seem unfavorable, do not hesitate to seek clarification from the lender or consult with a financial advisor. Negotiating terms is also an option, especially if you have multiple offers to consider. Choose the loan that best aligns with your financial goals and provides the most favorable terms for your business.

Crowdfunding Strategies
Crowdfunding has revolutionized the way entrepreneurs and small business owners raise capital. By leveraging the power of the internet and social networks, crowdfunding allows you to reach a broad audience of potential investors and supporters. Whether you're launching a new product, expanding your business, or funding a creative project, a well-executed crowdfunding campaign can provide not only the financial support you need but also valuable market validation and customer engagement. The key to a successful campaign lies in strategic planning, compelling storytelling, and effective promotion.

The first step in crafting a successful crowdfunding campaign is to select the right platform for your project. Numerous crowdfunding platforms cater to different types of projects and industries. Kickstarter and Indiegogo are among the most popular, offering a wide range of categories from technology to arts. For equity crowdfunding, platforms like SeedInvest and Crowdcube allow backers to invest in exchange for equity in your company. Research each platform's audience, fee structure, and success rates to determine which aligns best with your goals and target demographic.

Once you've chosen a platform, it's essential to set clear, realistic goals for your campaign. Define the amount of money you need to raise and what it will be used for. This goal should be specific and justifiable, providing potential backers with a clear understanding of how their contributions will be utilized. Avoid setting overly ambitious targets that may be difficult to achieve, as failing to meet your goal can harm your project's credibility and momentum. Break down your funding needs into tangible milestones, and communicate these clearly to your audience.

A compelling pitch is the heart of your crowdfunding campaign. Your pitch should tell a captivating story that resonates with potential backers. Start by explaining the problem your product or project addresses and why it matters. Personalize your narrative by sharing your journey, the challenges you've faced, and your passion for finding a solution. Use a mix of text, images, and videos to create an engaging and visually appealing presentation. A well-produced video can significantly enhance your pitch by conveying emotion and building a personal connection with your audience. Keep your video concise, ideally between two to three minutes, and focus on the most critical aspects of your story.

In addition to a strong narrative, your pitch should highlight the unique value proposition of your product or project. Clearly articulate what sets your offering apart from existing solutions and why backers should support it. Provide detailed information about the features, benefits, and potential impact of your product. If applicable, showcase prototypes, design concepts, or user testimonials to build credibility and demonstrate progress. Transparency is crucial; be honest about your project's current status, potential risks, and how you plan to overcome them.

Rewards and incentives play a vital role in attracting backers to your campaign. Offer a range of reward tiers that cater to different levels of contribution, from small tokens of appreciation to exclusive, high-value perks. Ensure that your rewards are meaningful, relevant to your project, and deliverable within a reasonable timeframe. Limited-edition items, early access to products, and personalized experiences can be particularly appealing. Clearly outline the delivery timeline for each reward, and keep your promises to maintain trust and satisfaction among your backers.

Promotion is another critical component of a successful crowdfunding campaign. Building awareness and driving traffic to your campaign page requires a multifaceted approach. Start by leveraging your existing network of friends, family, and colleagues. Personal endorsements from people who know and trust you can significantly boost your campaign's credibility and reach. Utilize social media platforms to share your story, engage with potential backers, and create buzz around your campaign. Regular updates, behind-the-scenes content, and interactive posts can help maintain interest and momentum.

Email marketing is another powerful tool for promoting your campaign. Build and segment your email list to target different groups of potential backers, such as previous customers, industry influencers, and media contacts. Craft personalized and compelling email messages that highlight the most exciting aspects of your project and encourage recipients to support and share your campaign. Timing is crucial; plan your email outreach to coincide with key milestones, such as the campaign launch, mid-campaign updates, and the final push before the deadline.

Media coverage can provide a significant boost to your crowdfunding campaign by reaching a broader audience and adding credibility. Develop a press kit that includes a press release, high-quality images, and background information about your project. Reach out to journalists, bloggers, and influencers in your industry with personalized pitches that explain why your project is newsworthy and relevant to their audience. Be prepared to offer interviews, provide additional information, and accommodate their schedules to maximize your chances of securing coverage.

Engaging with your backers throughout the campaign is essential for building a strong community and fostering long-term support. Respond promptly to comments and questions on your campaign page, social media, and other communication channels. Show appreciation for your backers' contributions and keep them informed about your project's progress with regular updates. Transparency and open communication can help build trust and encourage backers to become advocates for your campaign.

Once your campaign is successfully funded, the real work begins. Fulfilling your promises and delivering your rewards on time is crucial for maintaining the trust and satisfaction of your backers. Create a detailed project timeline that outlines the steps needed to complete your project and deliver rewards. Communicate this timeline to your backers and update them regularly on your progress. If you encounter any delays or challenges, be transparent and honest about the situation, explaining how you plan to address the issues and providing revised timelines if necessary. Backers are generally understanding if they are kept in the loop and see that you are making a concerted effort to overcome obstacles.

Managing Cash Flow and Budgets
Effective cash flow and budget management are the cornerstones of a successful business. Without a firm grasp on these financial aspects, even the most innovative and promising ventures can quickly find themselves in trouble. To ensure your business

remains solvent and profitable, it's crucial to understand how to track, analyze, and optimize your cash flow and budgets. This chapter will guide you through practical strategies and actionable advice to help you manage your business finances with precision and confidence.

Cash flow represents the movement of money in and out of your business. It encompasses all income generated from sales, investments, and other sources, as well as all expenses such as operational costs, salaries, and loan repayments. Positive cash flow indicates that your business is earning more than it spends, which is essential for growth and sustainability. Negative cash flow, on the other hand, can signal potential financial distress and needs prompt attention.

To effectively manage cash flow, start by developing a cash flow forecast. This forecast is a detailed projection of your expected cash inflows and outflows over a specific period, typically a month, quarter, or year. Begin by listing all anticipated sources of income, including sales revenue, investment returns, and any other forms of income. Next, outline all expected expenses, such as rent, utilities, payroll, and inventory costs. By comparing these projections, you can identify periods where you might experience cash shortages and take proactive measures to address them.

One of the most critical aspects of cash flow management is ensuring timely invoicing and collections. Delayed payments from customers can severely disrupt your cash flow, so it's essential to establish clear payment terms and follow up promptly on overdue invoices. Consider implementing an invoicing system that automates the process and sends reminders to clients. Offering incentives for early payments or penalties for late payments can also encourage timely settlements.

Another key strategy is to manage your expenses carefully. Regularly review your operating costs and identify areas where you can cut unnecessary expenses or negotiate better terms with suppliers. Implementing cost-saving measures, such as energy-efficient practices or outsourcing non-core tasks, can also help improve your cash flow. Additionally, maintaining a reserve of cash or a line of credit can provide a safety net during periods of low cash flow or unexpected expenses.

Budgeting is another fundamental tool for managing your business finances. A budget is a financial plan that outlines your expected income and expenses over a specific period. It serves as a roadmap for your financial activities and helps you allocate resources effectively. To create a realistic budget, start by reviewing your historical financial data and identifying trends in your income and expenses. Use this information to set reasonable targets and allocate funds accordingly.

Once your budget is in place, it's crucial to monitor it regularly and adjust as needed. Compare your actual income and expenses to your budgeted figures to identify any variances. Analyzing these discrepancies can help you understand the reasons behind them and make informed decisions to stay on track. For instance, if you notice that your operational costs are consistently higher than budgeted, investigate the underlying causes and explore ways to reduce them.

Another critical aspect of budgeting is prioritizing your spending. Not all expenses are created equal, and it's essential to distinguish between essential and non-essential costs. Focus on allocating funds to areas that directly contribute to your business's growth and sustainability, such as product development, marketing, and customer service. By prioritizing your spending, you can ensure that your resources are used efficiently and effectively.

Cash flow and budget management also require a keen understanding of your business's financial health. Regularly reviewing your financial statements, such as the balance sheet, income statement, and cash flow statement, can provide valuable insights into your business's performance. These statements offer a comprehensive view of your assets, liabilities, revenue, and expenses, helping you identify trends, strengths, and areas for improvement.

In addition to internal financial reviews, consider seeking external advice from financial experts or mentors. An experienced accountant or financial advisor can provide valuable guidance on managing your cash flow and budgets, helping you make informed decisions and avoid common pitfalls. They can also assist with financial forecasting, tax planning, and identifying opportunities for growth and cost savings.